The Man In The High-Water Boots

Francis Hopkinson Smith

Writat

Diese Ausgabe erschien im Jahr 2023

ISBN: 9789359254722

Herausgegeben von
Writat
E-Mail: info@writat.com

THE MAN IN THE HIGH-WATER BOOTS

By F. Hopkinson Smith

down in his automobile—a long, low, double-jointed crouching tiger—a forty-devil-power machine, fearing neither God nor man, and which is bound sooner or later to come to an untimely end and the scrap heap.

All about, fringing the tea tables and filling the summer air with their chatter and laughter, were gathered not only the cream, but the very top skimmings of all the fashion and folly of Trouville—twenty minutes away, automobile time—their blossoming hats, full-blown parasols, and pink and white veils adding another flower-bed to the quaint old courtyard.

With the return of the Man from the Latin Quarter, his other guest, who knew the ins and outs of the cellar, and who had gone in search of a certain vintage known only to the initiated (don't forget to ask for it when you go—it has no label, but the cork is sealed with yellow wax; M. Ramois, the good landlord, will know the kind—*if he thinks you do*), our host, the Sculptor, his mind still on his friend the painter, looked up and said, as he reached for the corkscrew:

"Why not go to-morrow? The mill is the most picturesque thing you ever saw—an old Louis XIII house and mill on the River Rille near Beaumont-le-Roger, once inhabited by the poet Chateaubriand. The river runs underground in the sands for some distance and comes out a few miles from Knight's— cold as ice and clear as crystal and packed full of trout. Besides Knight is at home—had a line from him this morning."

The Man from the Quarter laid down his glass.

"How far is it?" This man is so daft on fishing that he has been known to kiss the first trout he hooks in the spring.

"Only fifty-six miles, my dear boy—run you over in an hour."

"And everything else that gets in the way," said the Man from the Quarter, moving his glass nearer the Sculptor's elbow.

"No danger of that—I've got a siren that you can hear for a mile—but really, it's only a step."

I once slid down a salt mine on a pair of summer pantaloons and brought up in total darkness (a godsend under the circumstances). I still shudder when I think of the speed; of the way my hair tried to leave my scalp; of the peculiar blink in my eyes; of the hours it took to live through forty seconds; and of my final halt in the middle of a moon-faced, round-paunched German who was paid a mark for saving the bones and necks of idiots like myself.

This time the sliding was done in an overcoat (although the summer sun was blazing), a steamer cap, and a pair of goggles. First there came a shivery chuggetty-chug, as if the beast was shaking himself loose. Next a noise like the opening of a bolt in an iron cage, and then the Inn of William the Conqueror—the village-beach, inlet—wide sea, streamed behind like a panorama run at high pressure.

The first swoop was along the sea, a whirl into Houlgate, a mad dash through the village, dogs and chickens running for dear life, and out again with the deadly rush of a belated wild goose hurrying to a southern clime. Our host sat beside the chauffeur, who looked like the demon in a ballet in his goggles and skull-cap. The Man from the Quarter and I crouched on the rear seats, our eyes on the turn of the road ahead. What we had left behind, or what might be on either side of us was of no moment; what would come around that far-distant curve a mile away and a minute off was what troubled us. The demon and the Sculptor were as cool as the captain and first mate on the bridge of a liner in a gale; the Man from the Quarter stared doggedly ahead; I was too scared for scenery and too proud to ask the Sculptor to slow down, so I thought of my sins and slowly murmured, "Now I lay me."

When we got to the top of the last hill and had swirled into the straight broad turnpike leading to Lisieux, the Sculptor spoke in an undertone to the demon, did something with his foot or hand or teeth—everything with which he could push, pull, or bite was busy—and the machine, as if struck by a lash, sprang into space. Trees, fences, little farmhouses, hay-stacks, canvas-covered wagons, frightened children, dogs, now went by in blurred outlines; ten miles, thirty miles, then a string of villages, Liseau among them, the siren shrieking like a lost soul sinking into perdition.

"Watch the road to the right," wheezed the Sculptor between his breaths; "that is where the Egyptian prince was killed—" this over his shoulder to me—"a tram-car hit him—you can see the hole in the bank. Made that last mile in sixty-five seconds—running fifty-nine now—look out for that cross-road—'Wow-wow-oo—wow-wow'" (siren). "Damn that market cart—'Wow-wow-o-o-wow.'" "Slow up, or we'll be on top of that donkey—just grazed it. Can't tell what a donkey will do when a girl's driving it." 'Wow-oo-w-o—.'

Up a long hill now, down into a valley—the road like a piece of white tape stretching ahead—past school-houses, barns, market gardens; into dense woods, out on to level plains bare of a tree—one mad, devilish, brutal rush, with every man's eyes glued to the turn of the road ahead, which every half minute swerved, straightened, swerved again; now blocked by trees, now opening out, only to close, twist, and squirm anew. Great fun this, gambling with death, knowing that from behind any bush, beyond every hill crest, and around each curve there may spring something that will make assorted junk of your machine and send you to Ballyhack!

"Only one more hill," breathed the Sculptor, wiping the caked dust from his lips. Woo-oo-wow-o-o (nurse with a baby-carriage this time, running into the bushes like a frightened rabbit). "See the mill stream—that's it flashing in the sunlight! See the roof of the mill? That's Aston Knight's! Down brakes! All out—fifty-six miles in one hour and twenty-two minutes! Not bad!"

I sprang out—so did the Man from the Quarter—the flash from the mill stream glistening in the sunlight had set his blood to tingling; as for myself, no sheltering doorway had ever looked so inviting.

"Marie! *Marie!* Where's monsieur?" cried out the Sculptor from his seat beside the demon.

"Up-stairs, I think," answered a stout, gray-haired, rosy-cheeked woman, wiping her hand and arms on her apron as she spoke. She had started on a run from the brook's edge behind the house, where she had been washing, when she heard the shriek of the siren, but the machine had pulled up before she could reach the door-step.

"He went out early, but I think he's back now. Come in, come in, all of you. I'm glad to see you—so will he be."

Marie was cook, housemaid, valet, mother, doctor, and any number of things beside to Knight; just as in the village across the stream where she lived—or rather slept o' nights—she was billposter, bell-ringer, and town crier, to say nothing of her being the mother of eleven children, all her own—Knight being the adopted twelfth.

"The mill might as well be without water as without Marie," said the Sculptor. "Wait until you taste her baked trout—the chef at the Voisin is a fool beside her." We had all shaken the dear woman's hand how and had preceded her into the square hall filled with easels, fresh canvases, paintings hung on hooks to dry, pots of brushes, rain coats, sample racks of hats, and the like.

All this time the beast outside was snorting like a race-horse catching its breath after a run, the demon walking in front of it, examining its teeth, or mouth, or eyes, or whatever you do examine when you go poking around in front of it.

Up the narrow stairs, now in single file, and into a bedroom—evidently Knight's—full of canvases, sketching garb, fishing-rods and reels lining the walls; and then into another—evidently the guest's room—all lace covers, cretonne, carved chests, Louis XVI furniture, rare old portraits, and easy-chairs, the Sculptor opening each closet in turn, grumbling, "Just like him to try and fool us," but no trace of Knight.

Then the Sculptor threw up a window and thrust out his head, thus bringing clearer into view a stretch of meadow bordered with clumps of willows shading the rushing stream below.

"Louis! *Louis!* Where the devil are you, you brute of a painter?"

There came an halloo—faint—downstream.

"The beggar's at work somewhere in those bushes, and you couldn't get him out with dynamite until the light changed. Come along!"

There's no telling what an outdoor painter will submit to when an uncontrollable enthusiasm sweeps him off his feet, so to speak. I myself barely held my own (and within the year, too) on the top step of a crowded bridge in Venice in the midst of a cheering mob at a regatta, where I used the back of my gondolier for an easel, and again, when years ago, I clung to the platform of an elevated station in an effort to get, between the legs and bodies of the hurrying mob, the outlines of the spider-web connecting the two cities. I have watched, too, other painters in equally uncomfortable positions (that is, out-of-door painters; not steam-heated, easy-chair fellows, with pencil memoranda or photos to copy from) but it was the first time in all my varied experiences that I had ever come upon a painter standing up to his armpits in a swift-flowing mill or any other kind of stream, the water breaking against his body as a rock breasts a torrent, and he working away like mad on a 3 x 4 lashed to a huge ladder high enough to scale the mill's roof.

"Any fish?" yelled the Man from the Quarter.

"Yes, one squirming around my knees now—shipped him a minute ago—foot slipped. Awful glad to see you—stay where you are till I get this high light."

"Stay where I am!" bellowed the Sculptor. "Do you think I'm St. Peter or some long-legged crane that—"

"All right—I'm coming."

He had grabbed both sides of the ladder by this time, and with head in the *crotch* was sloshing ashore, the water squirting from the tops of his boots.

"Shake! Mighty good of you fellows to come all the way down to see me. Here, you stone-cutter—help me off with these boots. Marie's getting luncheon. Don't touch that canvas—all this morning's work—got to work early." (It looked to be a finished picture to me.)

He was flat on the grass now, his legs in the air like an acrobat about to balance a globe, the water pouring from his wading boots, soaking the rest of him, all three of us tugging away—I at his head, the Sculptor at his feet. How Marie ever helped him squirm out of this diving-suit was more than I could tell.

We had started for the mill now, the Man from the Quarter lugging the boots, still hoping there might be some truth in the trout story, the Sculptor with the palette (big as a tea-tray), Knight with the ladder, and I with the wet canvas.

Again the cry rang out: "Marie! *Marie!*" and again the old woman started on a run—for the kitchen this time (she had been listening for this halloo—he generally came in wringing wet)—reappearing as we reached the hall door, her apron full of clothes swept from a drying line stretched before the big, all-embracing fireplace. These she carried ahead of us upstairs and deposited on the small iron bedstead in the painter's own room, Knight close behind, his wet socks making Man-Friday footprints in the middle of each well-scrubbed step. Once there, Knight dodged into a closet, wriggled himself loose, and was out again with half of Marie's apronful covering his chest and legs.

It was easy to see where the power of his brush lay. No timid, uncertain, niggling stroke ever came from that torso or forearm or thigh. He hewed with a broad axe, not with a chisel, and he hewed true—that was the joy of it. The men of Meissonier's time, like the old Dutchmen, worked from their knuckle joints. These new painters, in their new technique— new to some—old really, as that of Velasquez and Frans Hals—swing their brushes from their spinal columns down their forearms (Knight's biceps measure seventeen inches) and out through their finger-tips, with something of the rhythm and force of an old-time blacksmith welding a tire. Broad chests, big boilers, strong arms, straight legs, and stiff backbones have much to do with success in life—more than we give them credit for. Instead of measuring men's heads, it

"The soaking is what helps," replied Knight, reaching for a match. "I like to feel I'm drink-some of it in. Then, when you're right in the middle of it you don't put on any airs and try to improve on what's before you and spoil it with detail. One dimple on a girl's cheek is charming; two—and you send for the doctor. And she's so simple when you look into her face—I'm talking of the brook now, not the girl—and it's so easy to put her down as she is, not the form and color only, but the *mood* in which you find her. A brook is worse, really, than your best girl in the lightning changes she can go through—laughing, crying, coquetting—just as the mood seizes her. There, for instance, hanging over your head is a 'gray day'"—and he pointed to one of his running-water sketches tacked to the wall. "I tried to cheer her up a little with touches of warm tones here and there—all lies—same kind you tell your own chickabiddy when she's blue—but she wouldn't have it and cried straight ahead for four hours until the sun came out; but I was through by that time and waded ashore. You can see for yourselves how unhappy she was." He spoke as if the sketch was alive—and it was.

"But I always work out of doors that way," he continued. "In winter up in Holland I sit in furs and wooden shoes, and often have to put alcohol in my water-cups to keep my colors from freezing. My big picture of 'The Torrent'—the one in the Toledo Art Gallery—was painted in January, and out of doors. As for the brushwork, I try to do the best I can. I used to tickle up things I painted; some of the fellows at Julian's believed in that, and so did Fleury and Lefebvre to some extent."

"And when did you get over it?" I asked.

"When my father persuaded me to send a bold sketch to the Volney Club, which I had done to please myself, and which they hung and bought. So I said to myself: 'Why trim, clean up, and make pretty a picture, when by simply painting what I love in nature in a free, breezy manner while my enthusiasm lasts—and it generally lasts until I get through;—sometimes it spills over to the next day—I please myself and a lot of people beside."

We were all on our feet now examining the sketches—all running-brook studies—most of them made in that same pair of high-water boots. No one but the late Fritz Thaulow approaches him in giving the reality of this most difficult subject for an outdoor painter. The ocean surf repeats itself in its recurl and swash and by close watching a painter has often a chance to use his "second barrel," so to speak, but the upturned face of an unruly brook-is not only million-tinted and endless in its expression, but so sensitive in its reflections that every passing cloud and patch of blue above it saddens or cheers it.

"Yes, painting water is enough to drive you mad," burst out Knight, "but I don't intend to paint anything else—not for years, any way. Hired the mill so I could paint the water running *away* from you downhill. That's going to take a good many years to get hold of, but I'm going to stick it out. I can't always paint it from the banks, not if I want to study the middle ripples at my feet, and these are the ones that run out of your canvas just above your name-plate. *Got* to stand in it, I tell you. Then you get the drawing, and the drawing is what counts. Oh, I love it!" Knight stretched his big arms and legs and sprang from his chair.

"Really, fellows, I don't know anything about it. All I do is to let myself go. I always *feel* more than I *see*, and so my brush has a devil of a job to keep up. Marie! *Marie!*"

Had the good woman been a mile down the brook she could have heard him—she was only in the next room. "Bring in the boots—two pairs this time—we're going fishing. And, Marie—has the chauffeur had anything to eat?"

"Yes, monsieur."

"Anything to drink?"

"No, monsieur."

"*What!* Hand him this," and he grabbed a half-empty bottle from the table.

I sprang forward and caught it before Marie got her fingers around it.

"Not if I know it!" I cried. "We've got to get back to Dives. When he lands me inside my garden at the inn he shall have a magnum, but not a drop till he does."

When the two had gone the Sculptor and I leaned back in our chairs and lighted fresh cigars. My enthusiasm has not cooled for the sports of my youth. With a comfortable stool, a well-filled basket, and a long jointed rod, I, like many another staid old painter, can still get an amazing amount of enjoyment watching a floating cork, but I didn't propose to follow those two lunatics. I knew the Man from the Quarter—had known him from the day of his birth—and knew what he would do and where he would go (over his head sometimes) for a poor devil of a fish half as long as his finger, and I had had positive evidence of what the other web-footed duck thought of ice-cold water. No, I'd take a little sugar in mine, if you please, and put a drop of—but the Sculptor had already foreseen and was then forestalling my needs, so we leaned back in our chairs once more.

Again the talk covered wide reaches.

"Great boy, Knight," broke out the Sculptor in a sudden burst of enthusiasm over his friend. "You ought to see him handle a crowd when he's at work. He knows the French people—never gets mad. He bought a calf for Marie last week, and drove it home himself. Told me it had ten legs, four heads, and twenty tails before he got it here. Old woman lost hers and Knight bought her another—he'd bring her a herd if she wanted it. All the way from the market the boys kept up a running fire of criticism. When the ringleader came too near, Knight sprang at him with a yelp like a dog's. The boy was so taken aback that he ran. Then Knight roared with laughter, and in an instant the whole crowd were his friends—two of them helped him get the calf out of town. When a French crowd laughs with you you can do anything with them. He had had more fun bringing home that calf, he told me, than he'd had for weeks, and he's a wonder at having a good time."

Then followed—much of which was news to me—an account of the painter's earlier life and successes.

He was born in Paris, August 3, 1873; his father, Ridgway Knight, the distinguished painter, and his mother, who was Rebecca Morris Webster, both being Philadelphians. Not only is he, therefore, of true American descent, but his eight great-grandparents were Americans, dating back to Thomas Ridgway, who was born in Delaware in 1713. Thus by both the French and American laws he is an American citizen.

At fourteen he was sent to Chigwell School in England by his father, to have "art knocked out of him" by the uncongenial surroundings of the quiet old school where the great William Penn had been taught to read and write. He left in 1890, having won the Special Classical Prize, Oxford and Cambridge certificate Prize, besides prizes for carpentering, gymnasium, running, and "putting the weight."

At home the boy always drew and painted for pleasure, as well as at school during the half-holidays. Some water-colors made during a holiday trip in Brittany in 1890 decided his father to allow him to follow art as a career. He entered Julian's studio, with Jules Lefebvre and Tony Robert-Fleury as professors in 1891, and studied from the nude during the five following winters. His principal work was, however, done in the country at and around Poissy, under the guidance of his father.

His exhibits in the Paris Salon (*artistes Français*) were twenty-four oils and water-colors from 1894 to 1906, obtaining an honorable mention in 1901 with the "Thames at Whitchurch"; a gold medal, third class, in 1905, with "The Torrent"; and a gold medal, second class, in 1906, with his triptych "The Giant Cities" (New York, Paris, London), which makes him *hors concours*, with the great distinction of being the first American landscape painter to get two Salon gold medals in two consecutive years. He won also a bronze medal in the American section of the Paris Universal Exhibition in 1900 with a water-color, and a gold medal of honor at Rheims, Cherbourg, Geneva, and Nantes.

His most important pictures are: "The Torrent," 4 1/2 x 6 feet, owned by the Toledo Art Gallery; "The Abandoned Mill," 4 1/2 x 6 feet; "The End of the Island," 6 x 8 feet; "Clisson Castle," 3 x 4 1/2 feet, a water-color; "After the Storm," 3 x 5 feet; and "Winter in Holland," 3x4 feet.

I had listened to the Sculptor's brief account of his friend's progress with calm attention, but it had not altered my opinion of the man or his genius. None of it really interested me except that somebody beside myself had found out the lad's qualities—for to me he is still a lad. None of the jury who made the awards ever looked below the paint—that is, if they were like other juries the world over. They saw the brush-mark, no doubt, but they missed the breeze that came with it—was its life, really—a breeze that swept through and out of him, blowing side by side with genius and good health—a wind of destiny, perhaps, that will carry him to climes that other men know not of.

But what a refreshing thing, this breeze, to come out of a man, and what a refreshing kind of a man for it to come out of! No pose, no effort to fill a No. 8 hat with a No. 7 head; just a simple, conscientious, hard-working young painter, humble-minded in the presence of his goddess, and full to overflowing with an uncontrollable spontaneity. This in itself was worth risking one's neck to see.

Again the cry rang out, "Marie!" and two half-drowned water-rats stepped in; the Man from the Quarter in his underpinning—his pair of boots leaked and he had stripped them off—and Knight with his own half full of water. Both roared with laughter at Marie tugging at the huge white-rubber boots, the floor she had scrubbed so conscientiously spattered with sand and water.

Then began the customary recriminations: "Hadn't been for you I wouldn't have lost him!" "What had I to do with it?" etc., etc.—the same old story when neither gets a bite.

That night, bumping over the thank-you-marms, flashing through darkened villages, and scooting in a dead heat along ribboned roads ghostly white in the starlight, on the way back to my garden—and we did arrive safely, and the chauffeur had his magnum (that is, his share of it)—I could not help saying to myself:

"Yes, it's good to be young and bouyant, but it's better to be one's self."